Donor Conception Network

'Telling' and Talking about Donor Conception with people aged 17 and over
A Guide for Parents

By
Olivia Montuschi

Olivia Montuschi

Olivia Montuschi is the mother of two donor conceived adults, born in 1983 and 1986. She and her husband Walter Merricks founded the Donor Conception Network with four other families in 1993. Olivia trained as a teacher and counsellor and for many years worked as a parenting educator and trainer, writing materials and running parenting education programmes. She is the author of all the Telling and Talking booklets for parents of donor conceived children of different ages and has written many articles about parenting children conceived by egg, sperm and embryo donation. Olivia currently works part-time as Practice Consultant for DC Network.

Donor Conception Network

ISBN 978-1-910222-53-9

Published by the
Donor Conception Network,
154 Caledonian Road, London N1 9RD

Telephone: 020 7278 2608
email: enquiries@dcnetwork.org
www.dcnetwork.org

Please note that in the interests of member confidentiality, the photographs used on the cover of this and the Telling and Talking brochures are sourced from photo libraries for illustrational purposes only and do not necessarily portray families created through donor conception.

Contents

Acknowledgements and thanks

These materials would not have been produced without the financial backing of the Parenting Fund. This Government funding, administered through the National Family and Parenting Institute, is competitively provided for the voluntary and community sector in England to strengthen support services for parents. Very many thanks are due to those who took a chance and backed an unusual way of supporting parents.

I am enormously grateful to: Ken Daniels, Professor (Adjunct) of Social Work at the University of Canterbury, New Zealand; Marilyn Crawshaw, Lecturer in Social Work and Research Fellow at the University of York; and Jennie Hunt, Senior Counsellor at the Wolfson Family Clinic, Hammersmith Hospital, London, who painstakingly read and thoughtfully considered all four booklets. Their wisdom, knowledge and long experience of donor conception issues have immeasurably improved both the content and the way it is expressed.

The sections on child development have benefited greatly from Elizabeth Howell's depth of knowledge and experience of working with parents and children.

Janice Stevens Botsford, a donor conceived adult who has found some of her genetic siblings and discovered the identity of her donor, brought her compassion, thoughtfulness and passion for the truth to the booklet for parents of those aged 17 and over.

Marion Scott, Steering Group member of DC Network and mentor to How to Tell, made sure that the project kept on-track and provided invaluable support when I was flagging.

Sarah Gillam suggested the structure for the booklets and has edited and re-edited the texts with much patience.

Nothing would have been possible without the many families and individuals inside and outside DC Network who have talked with me in person, on the 'phone and by email about their thoughts, feelings and experiences of donor conception. It has been a privilege to hear your stories. Thank you for your permission to share them.

Lastly, but definitely not least, my thanks to my family, Walter, Dan, Will and 'Zannah. Your love, patience and support has kept me going.

Olivia Montuschi
April 2006

Telling and Talking
17+

"Telling her has released a sense of freedom in us both and reaffirmed our closeness." Chris, mum to an 18 year old daughter.

Introduction

This booklet is for people who have built or added to their family with the help of sperm or egg donation and are parents of someone over the age of 17 who does not yet know about their beginnings by donor conception. It assumes that for a range of reasons you are seriously thinking about or have already decided that you now want to tell your adult child (or children) about how they came to be part of the family and are looking for some guidance on how to go about this. If your child is 17 or 18 then you may also find it helpful to read the booklet for parents of 12 – 16 year olds as well.

The aim of the booklet is to help prepare and support you towards creating as positive a climate as you can when sharing this very personal truth about your family.

Over the next few pages you will find acknowledgement of your own possibly very mixed feelings, some practical suggestions about how you can prepare yourself for telling, and insights into the potential feelings and responses of your adult child or children. There is also guidance on setting the scene, language to use at the time of 'telling' itself and ideas on what can help afterwards.

Although infertility is the reason that most people need to use donor conception, some people, including one of the families featured, have done so in order to avoid passing on a genetic condition. The vast majority of this booklet is relevant for both situations.

The assumption made throughout the booklet is that at the time of conception you were part of a heterosexual couple; single women and lesbian couples having had to address the 'dad question' at an earlier stage. If, however, you are a solo mum, possibly with a child conceived by egg as well as sperm donation, or a lesbian couple contemplating sharing or adding to information about your family's origins with an adult child, you are likely to find many of the issues addressed and practical ideas given here helpful and adaptable to your situation. The main themes addressed are openness and honesty rather than the specifics of one family situation or another.

Throughout the text you will find stories of real families and quotes from donor conceived adults and sometimes their parents as well. Here is an introduction to some of the families that you will meet throughout the booklet so that you can refer back if necessary to understand their circumstances in the context of the section of the book you are reading. All names have been changed.

Phillipa is in her seventies and her husband is twenty years older. Their daughter Lucy, conceived by sperm donation because of her dad's infertility, was 37 when she was told that she was donor conceived.

Robert and Natalie are in their fifties. Their daughters Rebecca and Helena were conceived by sperm donation because of Robert's infertility. It is unknown if the donor was the same or different. Rebecca was 19 and Helena 23 when they were told of their donor conception.

Sheila and Derek are in their sixties. They are both carriers of a gene that was the cause of their second son's death in infancy. Their first son Dan, unaffected by the genetic disorder, was born before they conceived the child that died. Their two daughters Sarah and Nancy (different donors) were conceived by donor sperm as a way of avoiding having another child affected by the same genetic disorder. Nancy was 32 and Sarah a bit younger when they were told. Both women have since discovered that they are carriers of the gene. Nancy's husband is not a carrier (so their children are unaffected) and Sarah is not planning children yet but will make sure any future father of her children is tested.

Sylvia and John are in their late sixties. They had their sons Howard and Simon by sperm donation (different donors) because of John's infertility, probably caused by being a carrier of the gene for cystic fibrosis. There is a significant incidence of this genetically inherited disease in John's family. Simon was 40 and Howard 36 when they were told.

Deciding to Tell

Thinking about 'telling' is rarely an easy process. You would be unusual if you didn't have quite a mixture of feelings. Even if you had planned to 'tell' at this age, the very thought of talking now with your adult child may make your stomach lurch. But compared to the emotional energy you have had to spend over many years keeping the secret, deciding to tell may be a relief. And the message of this booklet is that although you can't prepare your offspring for this revelation, there is a great deal you can do to prepare yourself. One of the ways of doing this is talking things over with a counsellor, trusted friend or someone from DC Network. My husband and I sometimes see people at our home to help them think through their feelings and prepare to 'tell'.

Robert and Natalie are a couple who have been successful in business and in their personal life together. They have a good marriage and two adult daughters conceived by sperm donation whom they love very much. They came to see us because they felt there was a dissonance between the very loving and open relationships they had within their family and the withholding of the information about donor conception.

Phillipa had felt the burden of holding the secret for the whole of her daughter Lucy's thirty-seven years. She hated not being honest with Lucy but also wished to protect her elderly husband.

Your reasons for choosing to 'tell' now will be unique to your family. But it may be that, like Philippa above, you have been feeling the weight of the secret of donor conception for some time. It may also be that something has happened within your family or the wider world to make you feel that 'telling' has now become imperative or inevitable.

Sheila and Derek had turned to donor conception for their third and fourth child because, following the birth of a healthy child, their second son was born with a serious genetic disorder and died shortly afterwards. When one of their daughters married they realised that they would need to 'tell' because of the risk of her passing on the genetic disorder if she and her husband were both carriers. This daughter became pregnant before they had a chance to share the information and the pregnancy was a time of great anxiety for Sheila and Derek. The resulting child was unaffected but the increased anxiety proved a catalyst for bringing the importance of 'telling' to the top of their agenda.

Sylvia and John also found that it was a pregnancy in the family that finally pushed them into 'telling'. When their son Howard and his partner said they were going to have genetic counselling because of the presence of cystic fibrosis in John's family, Sylvia and John felt they could no longer postpone the day they had been dreading.

Other reasons that are causing parents of adult donor conceived people to re-visit the long held secret in their family are the prominence in the media of articles on the influence of genetics on an individual's health and the recent growth in the availability of DNA testing. For a relatively small sum a kit can be ordered on-line and once a sputum sample has been given and returned, the company will then give detailed information about genetic heritage and in some cases health risks as well. DNA testing is also taking place as part of the hobby of genealogy – tracing family trees – sometimes with unexpected results, as in the story below.

Hilary, an historian in her fifties, took a DNA test partly because her late father, in a pre-DNA testing era, had encouraged her interest in family history. To Hilary's shock she discovered a high percentage of an ethnic heritage that as far as she was concerned was not part of her family. Questioning of her mother led to the discovery that she and her two siblings all had different beginnings in life, hers being by anonymous donor conception. This revelation has caused extreme turmoil in the family.

When you attended your clinic so many years ago you will have done so at a time when the culture and climate in which donor conception took place was one of secrecy. The assumption then was that the best interests of all parties were served by no-one knowing that sperm or egg donation had taken place and that children did not need to know. Time has proved this to be false. Many adults who have found out that they have been conceived in this way have made it clear that they have a right to know and should have the same legal rights to information as adopted people, even if they choose not to follow them up. It is now realised that relationships in families can be affected in many ways by keeping the secret, not least because of the emotional energy that is taken up by doing so and the stress it can cause. Lelani Arris, an American donor conceived adult who did not learn of her beginnings until her thirties, had the following to say in an email to members of the Donor Sibling Registry in the US –

> "Secrecy is just plain bad in a family – looking back with the information I have now I suspect it may have contributed to the break-up of my parents marriage (they divorced when I was 11) and I know it caused some tensions between my mother and her sister (who were the only others who knew, and both felt I should be 'told'). It probably also introduced stress into my father's relationship with me while I was unaware of the reasons for it."

Since writing the first edition of this booklet in 2006 I have had contact with very many families preparing to tell their adult children about their beginnings. In preparation for updating the text I re-contacted some of the families my husband and I had worked with over the years. Without exception the parents spoke of the burden of carrying the secret, the huge anxiety around 'telling' and the massive relief once they had done so. I also spoke to the adult children of four of these families and their responses will be quoted at points throughout the text. There are also stories and quotes from other donor conceived adults, all told of their origins after the age of 18.

You may well be wishing that you had decided to 'tell' earlier but remember that nearly everyone felt secrecy was the right option in those days. This booklet's aim is to support you and help you prepare for telling your children now.

Preparing to Tell

My experience over the years in talking to parents of adult children by donor conception is that their worst fear is of rejection by their much loved child or children and a change for the worse in relationships in the family. Neither of these things has happened in all the families my husband and I have worked with, but this may be at least partly because they wanted to get it right and sought help. They were willing to look at themselves and their own motivations as part of the preparation and to put aside their own feelings in order to be honest with their children.

Sometimes feelings of stigma and shame about infertility or the need to use donor conception remain even after all this time. A couple of the mothers I talked to said how very difficult it was for them to have sperm donation. Despite their partners consent to the procedure they had felt almost dirty and as if they had betrayed their partner. They had gone through with it because they so very desperately wanted to carry a baby and become parents. Of course discussion of feelings about donor conception was not seen as necessary in the early days and it is only since the Human Fertilisation and Embryology (HFE) Act of 1990 that counsellors have been present in clinics. Since that time understanding of the need to grieve the child that could not be before moving on to have the child it was possible to have, has advanced considerably. If you feel that there are mixed or difficult feelings of shame or stigma still lingering then it may be helpful to talk with a counsellor, close friend or someone at DC Network as part of your preparation for 'telling'.

Philippa's angst about holding the secret of her daughter Lucy's conception for 37 years was palpable when I spoke to her on the phone. She found the enormity of what she had to say to Lucy unbearably painful but afterwards she wrote saying, "Thanks entirely to your wonderful support and preparation – the preparation was crucial – I was able to be very steady and positive, having rehearsed what I was going to say out loud in the car, and memorised the seven points I wanted to make."

Donor conceived adults need their parents to be able to handle the range of complex and often quite strong feelings that result from having the facts of their conception revealed to them, no matter how old or mature they are. Parents who have faced their own difficult feelings and prepared themselves for the occasion of 'telling' are much more likely to be able to fully listen to their children's feelings and not need to focus on their own.

Being prepared allows for more successful, constructive and open communication amongst family members in the future.

Loss and Fertility

You will have used donor conception to create your family because of a loss – a loss of the fertility of one of you individually and of both of you as a couple, plus of course of the child you hoped you could have together. What is sometimes hard for parents to hear is that your child may in turn experience a loss as a result of learning about being donor conceived. You will find more about the losses felt by offspring in the section on Reactions. We mostly associate the words loss and grieving with death. But death is not the only kind of bereavement. It is most helpful to grieve loss at the time that it is experienced but sometimes this is not possible and it is never too late to re-visit some of those feelings.

Recognising and acknowledging the losses involved for both you and your child can help you understand each other and work towards a new relationship free from the burden of secrecy.

Men's Losses

Sperm Donation

Being unable to make a partner pregnant can be felt as a great loss for a man. Fertility and sexual potency have long been confused in public perception and men have sometimes been the butt of cruel jokes about their (in)capacity to make babies. In the early days sperm donation was seen as 'the solution' to male fertility problems, but in masking infertility it invited an agreement to keep the secret that at the time was considered to be best for all. This was reinforced by the legal situation in the UK prior to 1991, where if the parents told the births registrar that sperm donation had been used, they could not put the father's name on the birth certificate and the donor had the legal status of father. The emphasis in those days was on rational and practical ways to create a child, at the expense of emotional considerations for either parents or child. Without the opportunity to discuss feelings and mourn the loss of their fertility many men were left feeling that their infertility was a personal failure and something to be ashamed of. Some men may still feel this way.

Egg Donation

Men whose partner has had egg donation often find that their focus has been on supporting their partner at the expense of allowing themselves their own feelings about the loss of a child who would have connected them. Sometimes quite strong feelings have been suppressed because of a wish to be able to fulfil the desire of their partner to bear a child. Men may have agreed to egg donation even though they themselves have not felt comfortable about it. They may possibly have insisted on secrecy about the donor assisted conception because of their complicated feelings; these being reinforced by the cultural climate at the time even though the legal situation changed after 1991, a time when egg donation began to be practised more widely.

Women's Losses

Egg Donation

Many women feel that being able to conceive a child is an essential part of what it means to be a woman. When it is discovered that this is not going to be possible using her own eggs, there can be a devastating loss of a sense of womanliness which, if it remains unexplored and grieved, can lead to a sense of being less entitled to be a true mother. The experience of pregnancy and birth can help restore some of this loss but some women may continue to feel fraudulent about their claim to motherhood right into child raising years, despite the day to day practical experience of mothering. Similar feelings may also be experienced by women who have used surrogacy.

Single women who would have preferred to have had a child with a partner have this loss to adjust to and those who have used egg donation as well as sperm donation have in addition the loss of genetic connection to their child. Whilst single women almost always tell their child about the use of sperm donation, talking about the egg donation as well is something that many solo mums find much more difficult and may only reveal later in their child's life.

Sperm Donation

Not being able to have the biological child of a much loved man is a great loss for many women. There is also a loss in keeping the information about infertility and any resulting treatment a secret as women are more likely than men to want to talk about it within their support network of family and friends. Women have sometimes offered to keep the secret against their better instincts, because they could see how hurt their partner was and wanted to protect him. Some women have even 'taken the blame' for fertility difficulties.

One of the greatest losses, however, for a woman may be that the keeping of the secret over the years has prevented conversations with her partner about feelings which could have led to them becoming closer and stronger as a couple. The other great loss is that, although a woman may have agreed to secrecy at the time, it has prevented a relationship of complete honesty with her child or children. Many of the parents, particularly the mothers, I have worked with over the years have expressed regret about the lack of honesty about donor conception in relationships with their children that were otherwise very open.

Talking with others as part of preparation for 'telling'

The information you are preparing to tell will belong to your child to share as they choose but you may feel that it would be helpful to prepare the ground first by telling other significant family members or friends. There may be people within the family or wider family/friendship networks that you know your child will turn to for support, so consider letting them know what you are planning to do. Involving someone who has the interests of your child at heart but is not immediately emotionally involved may be very helpful. There is a difference between others having known for a long time whilst your child remained unknowing, something that angers a lot of DC adults when they find out about it, and sharing the information immediately before telling in order to provide support for them.

> Philippa shared what she was about to do with Lucy's godmother Jean, someone she knew Lucy was close to. This worked very well for both mother and daughter as they both loved Jean and trusted her integrity and discretion.

Telling

You may want to construct and rehearse a 'script' for the occasion of telling, or you may be more comfortable allowing the words to flow naturally on the day. Alternatively you may feel you could best express yourself, to start with anyway, by writing a letter that your child could read in your presence or that you could read out loud to them.

With great trepidation Sheila and Derek sat their daughters down and told them that Derek was not their biological father. They then read together an account they had written out about what had led to their daughters being conceived by sperm donation while their older son had been conceived without help.

Robert and Natalie, though just as nervous as the couple above, chose to let the words flow on the day, telling the story between them equally and making sure they brought in the points they had agreed together beforehand.

It helps to be as confident as possible when you begin but whichever way you choose to do it, remember that you are starting to tell a story that will be ongoing and may lead to changes, potentially both positive and negative. Change usually causes discomfort at first but clearing the cloud of secrecy from the relationship is likely to be well worth it. All the parents I spoke to following 'telling' – sometimes several years later – said that they felt much easier in their relationships with their children following the revelation. As Sheila said to me,"I went from having thought about donor conception and how I was going to explain about it every day for years, to hardly thinking of it at all now."

It may be that both of you will be involved in telling your child or it may just be one of you for some reason. Whether the telling is done by one or both (and telling alone is discussed at greater length later in the booklet) the following guidelines have been put together following many discussions with donor conceived adults and their parents.

- **Offspring first** – put the emotional needs of your adult child first. It is the story of how they came to be part of the family. The story of your infertility can come later. Share information with all your children (including those who came into your family other than by donor conception) either at the same time or within a very short space of time.

- **Stage of development** – If your child is still a teenager, remember that this remains a very 'me' focused time in their lives. The older they are, the more they may be able to understand, eventually, your perspective and what you went through to have them. Allow them to come to this conclusion in their own time rather than talking about how difficult it all was for you.

- **Preparation** – think through what you want to say and why, including a clear but short explanation about why you have chosen to tell them now and not before. Don't be shy about talking it through with others first. Our experience is beginning to show that good preparation is one of the most important factors in limiting possible long-term damage to relationships when 'telling' in adult years.

- **Support** – make sure there is someone in place for you that you can share your feelings with afterwards. It could be a family member, friend or counsellor. This is particularly important if you are 'telling' alone. It is not fair to expect your offspring to bear the strong and/or difficult feelings you will undoubtedly have.

- **Timing** – try to choose a time when there are no other significant events going on in your adult child's life and make sure you have sufficient time after telling for any immediate responses, questions and discussion. Try not to make an appointment to 'tell them something important' as they are likely to assume you are about to announce a marriage break-up or serious illness. Instead, try to use a time when you would naturally be together, or, if they live elsewhere, invite them over for a meal or a drink.

- **Place** – home, yours or theirs, is better than a public place or a holiday resort. Your child may well need to be able to retreat to a familiar space of their own or contact a partner or friend. Howard's immediate reaction on being told was to run into the garden and then drive round to see his oldest friend.

- **Language** – choose the words that convey what you mean in a straightforward way. Give information clearly and simply and don't forget to speak with warmth about how much they were wanted and how loved they are. Your children will remember the feelings of caring you gave them when you shared the truth, long after the facts have sunk in. The following is an example of how such a conversation could be started. It is easily adapted for egg donation.

"Mum and I have something we want to tell you. It's about how your birth made us a family. We always wanted to have children, but it turned out that this wasn't going to be possible using my sperm. With the help of a clinic we used sperm from a donor – someone we didn't know – to help make you. We couldn't believe how lucky we were when Mum became pregnant and when you were born we were both extremely happy. We loved you then and haven't stopped loving you since. I imagine this is a bit of a shock and I'm sorry we haven't told you before. When we went to the clinic they seemed to think that children didn't need to know…things have changed since then. It was hard to find the right time when you were growing up but we felt you had the right to have this information now."

- **One thing at a time** – give the basic information first and resist the temptation to heap more on them until they are ready. News like this takes time to sink in.

- **Acknowledge** – how your child might feel and show that you understand, without becoming defensive. Sentences beginning in the following ways can be helpful –

  "I imagine that….(this is pretty difficult to take in etc.)"
  "You may be feeling…(upset/angry that we haven't told you this before etc.)"
  "It would be very understandable if…(you had a lot of mixed feelings going round inside you about this etc.)"

- **Follow-up** – let them know that this is a safe subject to talk about and that you are willing to discuss anything at a mutually convenient time. It can be helpful to initiate a conversation within a couple of weeks or so, just to check out how they are feeling and their readiness to talk.

In order to prepare yourself for your child's reactions and response to the information you are planning to give them, you may also want to think about the following –

- How women and men feel about the telling
- The words to use when talking about the donor
- Issues around telling alone

Men and 'Telling'

Sperm Donation

Undoubtedly the parent who is not genetically related feels they have the most to lose in their child being told. Men in particular fear rejection (perhaps because they have not had the bonding experience of carrying the baby for

9 months) and may also fear exposing their infertility, especially if they have avoided acknowledging it over the years and feel that it brings them stigma and shame.

These feelings are very understandable given the cultural climate at the time of treatment, but they are not a reason for men to take a back seat when it comes to telling. Your children will need you and want you to talk with them. The experience of the vast majority of men who have talked with their children about family beginnings by donor conception is that rejection has not happened. All the men I spoke to when following up their 'telling,' took part in the process and their children confirmed to me separately that this was important for them.

In contrast to men's fear of rejection, children sometimes need reassurance from their dad or mum that they are loved even though they are not biologically connected. In response to a question about whether anything had been unhelpful at the time of being told, Linda said "…probably my dad not being open enough about it. I needed to talk to him about it too, but he would rather forget it happened. His way of dealing with it was to block it out, which wasn't very helpful to me when I needed reassurance from him."

Several years after being told, Linda still had issues that she needed to resolve with her father so she found an opportunity to talk to him.

"It was really difficult and tense, but after my dad understood that it was me who needed the reassurance from him, he was really understanding and couldn't believe I had harboured the thoughts for so long without speaking to him."

Far from rejecting him, Linda needed to know that her father loved her and saw her as his daughter.

Traditionally men have not found it easy to talk about their feelings or to seek help with painful emotional issues such as infertility and donor conception, especially when they have been suppressed over so many years. In wishing to do what is best after 'telling' men may need to be prepared to reassure their children of their love, even if their children appear to withdraw at first. Although it may be tempting to revert to not talking about it, it is likely that, like Linda, those who have been told may need their parents to take the initiative in bringing the subject up from time to time.

Gemma, who was told at age 26, told me how she wished very much that her parents would spontaneously raise the topic now and again. Her family are very loving but after finally 'telling,' her parents seemed to feel they had 'done their bit' and Gemma and her brother were left high and dry with their feelings. In contrast to this family, sisters Rebecca and Helena enjoy talking and sometimes joking about donor conception matters with their parents Robert and Natalie.

Women and 'Telling'

Egg Donation

Because of the losses detailed in the section on Women and Loss, as well as the advice given by clinics at the time, many women in the early days of egg donation (and surrogacy) decided not to tell anyone, least of all their child, about having used the egg of another woman to conceive. Like men who need the help of a sperm donor in order to become a parent, non-genetically connected women often fear rejection from their child once s/he knows about the egg donation. Despite having carried the baby for nine months and spending every day of their lives mothering since then, some women still carry in their hearts a fear of being found out as not being a true mother. If this is you, then know that, like the situation detailed above, your child may need as much reassurance from you that they are loved as your true daughter or son. You are their mother and they are highly unlikely to question your role but they may well need to know how very much they were wanted and are loved.

Sometimes women who have used egg donation come under pressure from their partners not to tell anyone about the method of conception. This is sometimes because they feel protective of their partner, not wishing her to be subject to the potentially prejudiced views of others. Or it can be because they themselves have some feelings of shame or stigma about egg donation. This can be very difficult if the woman herself would prefer to be open.

Sperm Donation

We have explored elsewhere how many women would have preferred to be open with their children about donor conception from the start, but instead agreed to keep the secret. This was often to protect their partner or because of the legal implications and attitude of society at the time or because they were advised not to tell. Others genuinely felt that there was no reason for children to know. Many women who felt like this have changed their minds since then.

One of the women who found accepting sperm donation difficult, had convinced herself for years that it hadn't really happened. She was brought up short when in adulthood one of her sons, studying genetics at university, began to take a great interest in family traits and likenesses. So many years later, talking about her feelings and having them understood and validated, was enormously freeing for her.

If you are one of the women who still feels uncomfortable about 'telling' and are not quite sure why, then talking with a counsellor, friend or someone from DC Network could be enormously helpful and make all the difference to being able to 'tell' without the burden of the complex feelings you may have been carrying for so long. Like the men who are reluctant to be part of the telling, women need to know that their commitment and involvement in the process is in their children's best interest and is likely to be hugely appreciated by them.

Language

Throughout this booklet the term 'donor' has been used to refer to the person who provided the sperm or eggs that enabled the building of a family. Using the word 'father/mother' by itself or 'real father/mother' to refer to the sperm or egg provider can confuse the role of the donor with that of the person who has loved and actively mothered or fathered a child over the long years of child raising. The donor is a real person who does have an undeniable genetic connection to the children he or she helped create. This man or woman deserves to be referred to with respect and gratitude, but they do not have an active parenting role.

Adult donor conceived people may go through phases of using different words to describe the person who helped to create them. Biological or 'bio' father or mother are often used or 'genetic parent'. Sometimes a nick name is given. The first two quotes below are typical of donor conceived adults who, whilst remaining very curious about the persons who helped create them, remain clear who their father and mother are.

> "When people ask, 'Who's your real father?' I pedantically stop them and say, 'My real father is the man who raised me.' That's real to me…there's a sperm donor and a parenting father and these roles both exist."
> Barry Stevens, The Offspring Speak

"My mum will always be my mum regardless of genetics"
Octavia in A Different Story…Revisited

> Hilary feels a little differently. In an email to me, she said she feels she has three parents and three heritages. She has a mother who performed the biological and nurturing role, her dad, who performed the nurturing role and her biological father who gave her fifty per cent of her genes. They are all equal in her eyes.

Doing the 'telling' alone

In an ideal world both parents would share news with their child about how they came to be part of the family. But there are many reasons why you may be contemplating taking this on alone. Maybe your partner has died and you now feel free to talk about something that he or she would have found embarrassing and difficult. You may be divorced or you and your partner may still not agree about 'telling' but you believe that this is something you have to do. Or there may be a situation, like the one Philippa found herself in, where her much older husband was in deteriorating health and she felt that insisting he take part in sharing information with their daughter was not something he could manage. Philippa wished very much that her husband could have shared the task, but with daughter Lucy contemplating a DNA test it could not be put off.

Whatever your situation, there seem to be two basic scenarios:

- *Either* you are free to make this decision alone because your partner is dead or has long lost contact with you and your child

- *Or* the person you went into parenthood with remains in contact and therefore needs to be consulted or their situation at least taken into account.

If you are free to undertake the telling alone, all the guidance offered here is relevant to you, but it is particularly important to take time to think through your own feelings first and find yourself a back-up team. It is possible that you will be on the receiving end of anger and other feelings that are all the stronger because your parenting partner is no longer around. Your response may be to feel angry or sad yourself. It is helpful if you can acknowledge these feelings but express them to a friend, family member or counsellor instead of to your child, who should not be expected to be your supporter.

If you are not free to undertake telling alone, again all the guidance here is relevant but this is a much trickier situation. Individual circumstances will vary enormously. If the adult child concerned has a relationship, no matter how remote, with your partner or ex-partner then this person has a right to be consulted or at the very least informed about your wish or intention to tell. It will be very important for you to think through very carefully your reasons for wanting to tell. These may be quite complex, particularly if you have had a rancorous divorce, but remember that from your child's point of view the only valid reason is that it is their need and right to have this information about themselves. All reasonable steps should be taken to involve and include the other parent in the preparation process, even if they are unwilling or unable to be present on the occasion of talking with their offspring.

Phillipa, mentioned above, drafted in Lucy's godmother, a psychotherapist, as a supporter for both herself and Lucy as well as spending time with a counsellor and then me on the phone to prepare herself for telling without her husband's knowledge. In the aftermath, she told some close friends who validated her decision to 'tell' alone. Lucy, age 37 when she was 'told' also completely understood that someone of her father's age, generation and health status was too frail to be made to face something he had avoided acknowledging all his life. Lucy's reaction to being 'told' will be included in the section on Reactions.

Phillipa's decision to 'go it alone' without her husband's knowledge, was based on the very particular situation in her family. In other families it can be a very high-risk strategy putting strain on the relationships in the family and essentially stopping the donor conceived person from telling others close to them. It also essentially continues the secret and comes with a good chance of accidental disclosure. Where offspring feel resentment towards the parent who is unaware, it is unlikely that they will keep the secret for very long, leading to an unplanned confrontation that benefits no-one.

Support, as sought by Philippa, from good friends, counsellors or family members who can give you time without needing their opinion to dominate, is highly recommended.

Reactions

You will be well aware by this point that the information you are planning to give is likely to be received with a range of strong and/or mixed feelings. All the suggestions for preparing to 'tell' are intended to support you in being able to acknowledge your child's feelings without crumbling or becoming defensive. The good news is that whilst first reactions may be powerful, openness to discussion on your part and the passage of time are likely to lead to an appreciation of each other's perspective. Your child may have many questions and wish that you had given them the information earlier, but there is also the potential that a different and closer relationship may develop as a result of there no longer being a secret between you.

As I said earlier, part of my preparation for updating this booklet was to go back and speak to the parents and children in families where my husband and I had helped prepare the couple to 'tell'. In four of the five families I heard exactly the same feelings from the five adult children I spoke to. They described shock, sometimes to the extent of feeling that they were watching a film or hovering above the events, but once this had passed, their first concern was for their parents – sadness that they had suffered so much because of the secret over the years, compassion for their non-genetic parent (in each case here, their dad) and in some instances an element of relief as it explained differences between siblings (with different donors) and between parents and children.

In the fifth family, the two brothers, Howard and Simon, felt very differently to each other. Howard will never forget the 2014 football World Cup. He was sitting on the floor watching a game when his parents called round to say they had a very urgent matter they needed to discuss with him and his wife. They then went ahead and told him about his conception using a donor. After his initial reaction of running into the garden and then going to see his friend James, Howard soon began to see his parents perspective. He and his wife live close to his parents, who play a big part in looking after their 18 month old son. Howard feels wanted and loved and is happy to tell people about his beginnings and joke about it.

Simon, who was 'told' separately to Howard because he lives a long way from his brother and parents, was not in the least surprised to hear that he was not genetically connected to his dad. He was 40 when given the information and wishes he had known earlier but the news, when it came, brought "a tidal wave of relief." He had always felt rather detached from his father's side of the family and felt a lack of connection to his dad and questioned himself about it. He probably decided to move so far away because of this. He now says he hardly thinks about it and admits that the relationship with his parents has probably improved a bit as a result of the truth being known.

Lucy, Philippa's daughter, talked to me six months after she had been told. She recalls a sense of calm as her world turned upside down whilst at the same time nothing changed at all. She felt great compassion for both her parents and spent a lot of time with her dad over the weekend she was told. In the months since, Lucy has had an increasing sense of having gained some inner strength from the knowledge of her donor conception. It was a relief to know that she does not have a predisposition to her father's medical problems but it has not changed how she feels about him at all. When I asked Lucy to what she attributes her calmness and positive attitude about the revelation her mother made those few months ago, she says it is because she always knew that she was completely loved.

Lucy's sense of being wanted and loved were shared by all the donor conceived adults I talked to whose parents had sought help to prepare for 'telling'. Even Simon said that his dad had been a good father and he would always be grateful to both parents for a stable upbringing. All of the parents I spoke to had different reasons for wanting or needing to 'tell' their children at the time they did. What they all had in common were marriages that had stood the test of time, a great love for their children and a wish to do – belatedly – what was in their best interest, and to this end they sought help.

On the basis of these conversations with both parents and adult children, some of whom were told up to five years ago, it would appear that late telling need not be the cause of lasting damage, either to the psyche of the individual concerned or to family relationships. Ken Daniels, professor of social work from New Zealand and one of the world's foremost authorities on donor conception families, has noted similar findings and will publish research to this effect later in 2017.

Of course initial compassion for parents may not last and can be followed by a more troubled period. It can also be a manifestation of children feeling a need to 'rescue' or 'protect' parents who may be perceived as vulnerable. Your reassurance that you are able to deal with your own feelings and don't need protection from theirs, may be helpful.

Not all donor conceived adults, however, are lucky enough to have parents who are able and prepared to put aside their own feelings in order to share information with their children under good circumstances and to continue to talk with them afterwards. Some parents have 'told' and then left their children to manage the consequences, refusing to discuss the matter further. Other offspring have found out, not by being told by their parents, but through blood tests showing a blood group that could not have been inherited from parents, or as a result of seeing their medical records, or finding documents relating to their mother's treatment in family papers. Worst of all, the secret has sometimes been revealed in a family row, as parents were divorcing or more recently as an unexpected result of DNA testing (more about this in the section on Searching for Genetic Connections). In all these cases shock has been followed by distress and trauma. Anger is likely to be directed at parents and also at The System, meaning the way in which information about donor conception has been handled historically, both officially and unofficially, blocking the routes to people gaining information about their genetic heritage.

There is a group of DC adults, some told of their origins early in life and some later, who appeared to be comfortable with the information for many years and then, sometimes as a result of having children themselves, have changed their minds, to a greater or lesser degree, about donor conception. Some feel that the deliberate separation of biological parents from their offspring is wrong and that donor conception should be outlawed; others call for a universal ban on anonymous donation and access to donors before the age of 18 if children want this. These feelings and changes of heart do not necessarily mean a rejection of their parents and many of these DC adults and their families manage loving relationships alongside this change in attitude to their means of conception. It is a timely reminder that thoughts and feelings can always change over time, but with good will and good communication, positive family relationships can be maintained.

The power of secrets

It will not just be the information itself that will have an impact, but also the fact that a secret has been kept for the whole of your child's upbringing. Genetic connections that have been taken for granted are now being revealed as not being so. This can be experienced as disempowering and as a betrayal of trust.

Bill Cordray, one of the oldest known donor offspring and now in his seventies, says, "It's not the conception that hurts us so much, it's the deception." Bill, who had always felt very different to his father, had to squeeze the information about his donor conception out of his mother. Part of him was relieved as he had fantasised that he might be the result of an affair she had had.

Recent research with donor conceived adults 'told' late is that anger is often directed at their mother, even if she is the genetic parent and the one who would have preferred to 'tell' sooner. It seems that a higher standard of truth is expected from mothers! It is also true that following divorce mothers usually have the main caring and contact role and are therefore more available. However, it has also been shown that if a mother is able to withstand and manage strong and/or difficult feelings and keep lines of communication open, then there is a good chance of stable family relationships being resumed once the first shock has passed.

If the non-genetic parent has been distant, cold or dismissive towards their child there is some evidence that donor conceived people may use the fact of non-genetic connection as the reason for ending the relationship or 'de-kinning' this parent once origins become known.

Sometimes, as with Simon's situation described earlier, there is a sense of relief as questions that have puzzled them over the years are answered by the news.

Interestingly several of the donor conceived people I spoke to said that whilst they were comfortable with the information themselves and had told work colleagues and friends made away from home, they did not feel they could talk about their origins with old friends made in their home area where their parents still live. It seemed they were trying to protect their parents from being the subject of local gossip and two said this outright. Sometimes, although the non-genetic parent has taken part in the telling, he or she does not want their side of the family to know about their infertility. Linda, whose story about needing reassurance from her dad was told earlier, is not able to be as publicly open as she would like about being donor conceived because her dad's family do not know about it. This has caused Linda some frustration over the years. Gemma, who is in a similar situation, believes it is wrong for parents to limit their children in this way and that they should be genuinely free to tell anyone if they choose to do so.

Other issues that may arise following the lifting of the long held secret, are questions of trust – 'Can I really believe you in the future?' and "What else haven't you told me?'. Both of these represent the loss of a possibly previously unquestioned relationship. Time spent acknowledging feelings and answering questions willingly and honestly as they arise will go a long way to rebuilding trust, although it may be a rocky road for a while.

Who am I?

What makes us who and what we are? Just what is the role of nature and nurture in how we turn out? In modern times genetics seem to have come more to the forefront of people's thinking, partly because of publicity about developments in medical science and partly perhaps because in a fast moving and unpredictable world many people feel a need for the certainty of knowing their roots. Television programmes such as *Who Do You Think You Are?* and *Long Lost Family* both come out of and feed into this interest in genetic origins. For some donor conceived adults genetic connections, or their genetic family as they would put it, are enormously important. They feel they cannot know completely who they are without information about or preferably contact with the person who contributed their sperm or eggs to help make them. For others these links feel less important. They take their sense of self from their immediate family, education, work, friends and achievements – in other words see nurture rather than nature as shaping who they are. Parents cannot know how their child (young or adult) is going to feel about being donor conceived but evidence does seem to point to those who find out later rather than earlier and in poorer rather than planned circumstances, feeling more strongly about the loss of these genetic connections.

> Imogen in the study 'What does it mean to be a donor offspring' said "Part of me was shaken and profoundly shocked. Part of me was utterly calm, as things suddenly fell into place, and I was faced with an immediate reappraisal of my own identity."

Rebecca, one of Robert and Natalie's daughters, was 19 when she was 'told' and had recently been on a gap year in Israel, spending some time looking at questions of identity. She initially felt the connection with relatives on her dad's side had been weakened and wondered whether the donor was Jewish, the faith and culture she had been raised in. Five years later, when I talked with her, she said she would not ask these questions today. She has come to realise that genetics are not everything and her family's cultural Jewish influence is very strong.

Of course genetics and genetic relationships carry some influence on our place in the world – the story we tell about ourselves and the way we think about identity – for most of us. Where donor conception is involved there is added complexity because of lack of information for those for whom it is important and the feelings about the obstacles that are placed in the way of finding and making relationships with genetic relatives who may be seen as family members. Although some DC people say all they want to know is their donor's health history and genetic make-up, evidence is proving that the dominant interest seems to be curiosity about what sort of person their donor is/was in order to add this information to their story about who they are. Some donor offspring want to know whether they mattered to their donor – did that person consider that their donation would result in a human being? Others still feel that the method of conception is alienating, although many parents would claim that their DC children are born of great love, even if their conception did not take place in the time honoured way.

Of the seven DC people I talked to from the follow-up families, several were curious about genetic links. Simon, who felt so disconnected from his dad was one. Lucy said she would probably do a DNA test and search once her very elderly father had died. Sheila and Derek's daughter Sarah is a medical student and very interested in genetics. Her sister Nancy has already done a DNA test but without making any connections. None of them, however, feel that their donor is a parent or that having information about them would change how they think about their identity.

Hilary, who found out about her origins in her fifties feels differently. The knowledge about her donor conception has changed one hundred percent how she feels about her identity. As far as she is concerned her biological father is one of her three parents.

It is very normal for donor conceived people who learn about their origins as adults to have many questions about who they are and perhaps particularly who they look like, especially if they have not strongly inherited features from their genetic parent. The issue of physical likeness may well have come up in your family. Some donor conceived adults who do not fit with the physical, intellectual or creative characteristics in their family have asked if they were adopted or wondered if they were the result of an affair. Even though they are biologically related to one parent, they may still feel confused about where they fit in the family. Sylvia and John's son Simon felt this way.

Physical likeness seems to be important because it is seen as connecting families together over time. As human beings we establish who we are at least partly in relation to the people we are like over a range of characteristics. Our very tall blonde daughter would love to see her Scandinavian-style good looks reflected in someone else.

Adjusting to any new situation can take a while but if you have taken the time to prepare yourself, given the news in the best way you can and are willing to continue the conversation as and when your adult child needs it, you are doing everything you can to assist the process of integration of the news.

Siblings

If your child has grown up with brothers and sisters, then some of the first questions are likely to be about their relatedness to them. If you have other children by donor conception you may or may not know if they share the same donor. You may also have adopted children or have a child conceived without reproductive assistance. The revelation that brothers and sisters may not be fully biologically related can be a powerful one. Responses vary depending on the meaning of the information for the siblings involved, but it can be felt as devastating at first.

A young woman interviewed by Ken Daniels in New Zealand felt this way –

> "I was more gutted, and it sounds horrible, but I was more gutted that B wasn't my full sister. *(Laughs)* Oh my God we're not full sisters. And that really, really upset me."

But Stephanie, who emailed DC Network, felt that there was a more positive side too –

> "Getting my head around the fact that my sister and I have different donor fathers is mind boggling, although I think it's actually made our relationship even stronger."

Brothers Howard and Simon were always very different. Simon describes himself as ebullient and 'in your face' whilst Howard has always been quiet and diffident. It wasn't a surprise for them to discover they were half-siblings.

Sheila and Derek had a healthy son, Dan, without help before they had a child who died of a genetic disorder. Daughters Sarah and Nancy were conceived by sperm donation, probably from different donors, in order to avoid passing on the faulty gene. Neither of the women has had significant problems adjusting to their new knowledge but Dan, genetically connected to both parents, reacted to the information very differently. He was given the news a few days later than his sisters whilst on holiday with the family and his initial reaction was shock at the fact that his parents could have made such a choice and that he did not suspect anything. He felt he would not be able to choose donor conception for himself but once he knew more of the medical background to his parents' actions he quickly came to terms with it and retains warm relationships with the whole family.

Helena, one of Robert and Natalie's daughters, thinks that she and her sister share a donor, despite the fact that they look very different. The sisters are close and Helena didn't really want to think about the prospect that Rebecca might not genetically be a full sister.

There is another difference between these two. Rebecca was conceived after the Human Fertilisation and Embryology (HFE) Act 1990 so information about her donor and any half-siblings raised in other families will be on the Human Fertilisation and Embryology Authority's (HFEA) register. She could find out how many half-siblings she has, their years of birth and genders if she chose to do so. She could even register to be in touch with them by mutual consent. Helena, conceived before 1990 does not have these rights. So far Rebecca has chosen not to find out if she has half-siblings both inside and outside her family. This solidarity with her sister may or may not change with time.

Beyond the first overwhelming feelings, there are both advantages and disadvantages to a situation where siblings have been conceived by different donors. If, for instance, one sibling wishes to search for their donor and/or half siblings and the other does not, then it may be an advantage if they do not share a donor. But where both siblings wish for information, it may be more difficult if one is able to make a connection and the other is not. When siblings do share a donor it is important that their different needs for information are taken into account and respected, although this may be tricky to handle practically.

Where there are siblings conceived or brought into the family in different ways it will be important to value each of them for who they are and let them know they are loved equally. Following 'telling', all adult children, no matter how they were conceived, are likely to think back to how their parents have behaved towards them in the past.

Half-siblings

It may well be possible that you have never given a thought to the possibility of half-siblings – other people conceived with help from the same donor but raised in other families. I know my husband and I hadn't even considered the possibility until our daughter, aged 14, was asked how she felt about them by a journalist! Some donor conceived children and adults are more interested in these people than they are in their donor. Making connections with half-siblings can be less fraught than donor/offspring meetings and there is evidence from research studies in the United States that half-siblings have gained great satisfaction from having made contact with each other.

The donor

At some point following 'telling' your adult child is likely to ask questions about their donor. The sort of information they may be looking for can include non-identifying information such as medical history, physical characteristics and ethnic and cultural background, as well as more personal information about the donor's identity and personal traits. However, as I said earlier, it is becoming clearer that many donor conceived people want to know more about the donor's story, his or her motivations for donating and if they, the result of the donation, are ever thought about as people.

Most parents who had treatment in the UK prior to August 1991 when the HFE Act came into being, will have little information about their donor(s). My husband and I, in the early 1980s, were given nothing. Our doctor photographed us and said he would find someone who fitted with my husband's physical characteristics. Both our son and daughter are significantly taller than their dad but in photos we fit together as a family. There is no information whatsoever on which to base a search, something that is a cause of sadness for our daughter.

Searching for genetic connections

Until fairly recently finding out information about genetic relatives by donor conception was very difficult if not impossible in the UK. But the advent of relatively cheap DNA testing kits has revolutionised the possibilities for making these links and social media is connecting together the people who are searching. Further information about DNA testing is given below but these are the official routes for people conceived in the UK who are interested in trying to make connections with their donor or half-siblings.

As I said above in relation to sisters Rebecca and Helena, those people conceived in or after August 1991 will have their mother's treatment details, including information about the donor, and the outcome of treatment, recorded on the HFEA register. At age 18 those people conceived before April 2005, are able to find out non-identifying information about their donor, whether he or she has opted to lift their anonymity (most have not), the number of half-siblings, their years of birth and gender. All this information can be obtained by parents at any time before a child is 18. Young adults at 18 can also register to be in touch with half-siblings by mutual consent. People conceived after April 2005 will be entitled to identifying information about their donor from 2023 when the first cohort will turn 18.

For those conceived before August 1991, the Donor Conceived Register (DCR, formerly UK Donor Link) can help connect offspring to their donor or half-siblings via a DNA test taken from a sputum sample. This will of course only be possible if any of these people have also registered and given DNA samples. The DCR is a small government funded organisation that will be taken over by the HFEA in the autumn of 2017.

There is a private non-profit Donor Sibling Registry in the United States started by Wendy Kramer and her DC son Ryan. At the time of writing they were celebrating having made 14,000 connections between families linked via donor conception. Although this is mainly a US registry they do have sections for most countries in the world and it can sometimes be worth a UK based DC adult putting their information there.

DNA testing

Genetic connections can be made without the donor or indeed half-siblings having actually given a DNA sample and registered with one of the companies currently offering testing with kits bought from their internet sites. It only takes a close or distant relative of theirs to be interested in the genealogical history of their family for someone to be traced. Occasionally a direct link is made this way but usually it takes a little more detective work. However, there have quickly developed a number of Facebook groups to guide and support people in their search and individuals who specialise in genealogical linking. Whilst not everyone looking for their donor will be able find him or her, the chances of being able to do so increase every day. Bill Cordray, the American donor conceived adult in his seventies mentioned earlier, registered his DNA on several web sites and within a short time found out who his donor was via connections made through distant cousins of his donor in Norway!

Of course it is not just donor conceived people who have been told about their origins who are finding out information. Sometimes people are learning of their donor conception for the first time because they are contacted by a genetic relative or because they register with a site in order to gain health or genealogical history data, and then discover ethnic origin information that puts their genetic parentage in doubt. Hilary, mentioned at the beginning of this booklet, discovered the secret of her conception in this way after her father had died.

Knowing of the possibilities for DNA testing means that you and your child need to inform yourselves about the robustness of DNA links on these websites as DNA matches are based on a complicated analysis of markers indicating probability. There is more chance of error with half-siblings than with donor to DC individual. Many of the markers used are associated with genetic traits linked to health, so there may be the chance of unexpected news. Although your child will know they are donor conceived (once you have told them) they may discover half-siblings who have no idea they are also donor conceived or that their parent was a donor. Unlike discovering a donor or half-sibling via the Donor Conceived Register, there is no structure of support or mediation offered by these websites.

It can be shocking for parents of untold donor conceived people to realise that the secret they have kept for so many years can now be revealed in this way. If this applies to you, you may be feeling threatened by the thought that you could be confronted at any time by your daughter or son who has taken a DNA test. This booklet is of course designed to help you share information with your child or children in a planned and managed way before this potential event happens and to support you in understanding that initial shock followed by a need to know more is absolutely normal. However, searching can go underground. It is important that you are aware that it is not uncommon for DC adults to withhold the fact that they are searching, using official or unofficial routes, because they fear that this knowledge will hurt you. It may be worth taking the opportunity to reinforce that you will not be hurt by their wish to know more or take it as a rejection of you. It is good to ensure they know that you understand their curiosity and will react positively and respect their decisions regarding any links made (not forgetting that donors and half-siblings come with their own families and your child must negotiate for themselves what sort of relationships they want with any of these people).

As we have seen from the stories and quotes from donor conceived people and their parents throughout this booklet, some people feel a great need to find out as much as possible about their donor and half-siblings, some have less urgent curiosity and others still do not feel the need to search at all. What is important to recognise is that these feelings can change, either way, over time. Turning point events in donor conceived people's lives like getting married, having a child or the death of a parent can trigger more thought about genetic ancestry, and the likelihood or not of inherited diseases or characteristics being passed on. Feelings of sadness, anger or confusion may result. If you have kept a good connection with your adult child they may let you know what is happening for them. As when you first told them, good listening and support, without denial or defensiveness will help them through this time and hopefully lead to a calmer and happier place.

You may find it helpful to know that seeking and learning more about the donor or donor-related siblings rarely seems to be about looking for substitute family relationships. Research has shown that primary relationships with raising parents remain intact (sometimes following a temporary breakdown when first told) in families where relationships had mostly always been good anyway. In families where relationships had mostly been strained and difficult, donor conception might be named as the reason for a breakdown, although it is more likely that family dynamics played the largest part in this. A similar pattern is found in people adopted as infants – there has long been a myth that the only adopted people who search for their biological relatives are those who are unhappy in their adoptive families. The same accusation is sometimes levelled at donor conceived people who search. There is no evidence at all that this is the case. What they are looking for is further knowledge about themselves. It is not about rejection of you.

Final Thoughts

Making the decision that your adult child should have the information about how they came into your family has probably taken you beyond where you would usually feel comfortable emotionally. None of us likes to be in this place for very long. It is impossible to say how your individual child will take the news but DC Network does not know of any donor conceived people who would have preferred not to know.

This booklet has focused a lot on loss. This is because acknowledgement of loss is an important step in the process of re-assessing the decision you took so long ago. Deciding that secrecy may no longer be in the interest of your child or any of you is a big step. Hearing the truth may cause your children to feel an acute sense of loss themselves. Loss of what they always assumed to be true, loss of trust and for some, loss of genetic relatives. That this is so should not sway you from trying to tell the truth about their origins as best you can. The message from the families I went back to talk to was that taking that stomach churning leap and 'telling' was absolutely worth it. Parents felt supported by the preparation they had sought and hugely relieved that they did not have to live with the secret any longer. Offspring were mostly very respectful of their parents for having prepared themselves so well and compassionate about the agony they had felt about keeping the secret for so long. There was relief at the explanation of differences between parents and children or siblings (although these exist in genetically connected families as well) and pleasure all round in being able to talk openly about family characteristics and what features and traits might or might not have come from the donor.

As with all family stories, in the end it is not so much about what has happened but the way we are able to make sense of it that leads to being able to integrate it into part of who we are. If the story you tell your child is coherent and rings true (probably because of the emotion that accompanies it) it will be much easier for your child to take in and sooner or later see your perspective, alongside managing their own feelings.

Putting your children's feelings first is of course not always easy. Right at the beginning and as time passes your buttons are likely to be pushed by memories and issues your children might raise and need you to respond to. This can stir up old feelings of sadness, uncertainty and fear. Such feelings are absolutely normal and part of parenting (which as you will know does not stop once your children are adults). But they do need managing and this means facing and dealing with them rather than pushing them deep down inside and trying to ignore them. Be kind to yourselves. You have taken an enormous step by 'telling'. Continuing to acknowledge things you could have done better in the past can be helpful, listening to your children's feelings is more than valuable, but getting help and support for yourself is also important. Talking with your partner or a counsellor or finding a close confidante as Philippa did, can help sort out the things you need to face and deal with and what your child now really needs to do on their own.

Feelings of loss or confusion can come and go over the weeks, months and years for your children as well as for you. Sometimes they may feel fine and at other times they may not. Donor conceived adults may need independent counselling – somewhere they can express themselves completely honestly and confidentially – either in the first weeks after being told or sometime down the line. Your support in their need for this is likely to be welcomed.

Deciding to 'tell' is not without risk or anxiety, but many worthwhile things in life involve some risk-taking. After all, we grow as people as a result of making courageous choices. There is much to gain for everyone and Stephanie, whose mum Claire has the last word below, is clear that she is very pleased to have been told how she and her sister came into their family –

> "I think it's been really tough for my mum to have kept everything bottled up inside for so long. I know it was really hard to tell us after so many years and I think it took a lot of guts but I'm so glad that I finally know. She told us everything so beautifully and clearly that it's made it really easy to digest."

Claire sought support from DC Network before she took the plunge and shared the information about donor conception with her two daughters aged 21 and 23.

> "We were persuaded by the medical staff at the clinic that the way to approach the situation was to go home and forget that we had used AID. With that mind-set it was very difficult to think about the question of telling the children. I was always extremely unhappy with the situation and I knew it would be difficult to choose the moment for that life changing disclosure. In the end I opted for a time when everyone's life seemed relatively calm and, with a complete feeling of dread, I explained. They were shocked of course, but because they know that in everything else we have always been completely honest with each other, we were able to talk everything through and even to laugh. I really do have two amazing daughters."

Further Reading

Recent research referred to in the text of this booklet will be the subject of articles to be published after the April 2017 publication date of this updated booklet. One of the authors, Marilyn Crawshaw, is happy to be contacted for pdf copies of the papers, which otherwise would only be available via university libraries. The participants in the research are donor conceived adults and donors who registered with UK Donor Link, the organisation that held the UK pre 1991 register before the Donor Conceived Register took over.
Marilyn Crawshaw's email address is marilyn.crawshaw@york.ac.uk

- *Donor Conceived people's views and experiences of their genetic origins: A critical analysis of the research evidence*
  Eric Blyth, Marilyn Crawshaw, Lucy Frith and Caroline Jones
  (2012) 19 JLM 769

- *Finding Our Families: A First-of-Its-Kind Book for Donor Conceived people and Their Families*
  Wendy Kramer and Naomi Cahn
  Avery 2013)

Films

- *A Different Story* (Donor Conception Network, 2003) DVD
  Seven children and young people talk about their thoughts and feelings about being conceived with the help of anonymous sperm donors.
  Available for members to borrow from the DC Network library.

- *A Different Story...Revisited* (Donor Conception Network, 2014) DVD
  This DVD contains two short films. The first features children and young people from solo mother and lesbian families and the second children and young people from heterosexual couple families. All donation types are represented.
  Available to buy from DC Network or for members to borrow from the library.

- *Offspring* (2002) Video
  Made by professional filmmaker Barry Stevens, who was born as a result of sperm donation over fifty years ago. During his search for his biological father he unearths a half-brother who is also hoping to trace his past.
  Available for members to borrow from the DC Network library.

- *Sperm Donors Anonymous* (Sensible Films 2015) DVD
  This Australian made-for-TV documentary includes interviews with donors, donor conceived adults and one parent. It is very positive and well worth watching.
  Available for members to borrow from DC Network library.

- *Donor Unknown* (2010) DVD
  This American film is about donor conceived teenager Jo-Ellen Marsh's search to find out more about her sperm donor. On the way she discovers some half-siblings who come with her to visit their donor.
  Available for members to borrow from DC Network library.

Useful Contacts

Donor Conceived Register
www.donorconceivedregister.org.uk
The UK's official registry for donor conceived people and donors from pre 1991 era.

Donor Sibling Registry
www.donorsiblingregistry.com
A not-for-profit registry and Internet forum group started in 2000 by Wendy Kramer and her son Ryan in the US. It offers the opportunity for links to be made between genetic relatives by mutual consent without the use of DNA testing. Open to UK residents.

Human Fertilisation and Embryology Authority
10 Spring Gardens, St. James's,
London SW1A 2BU
020 7291 8200
www.hfea.gov.uk
The UK's official regulator for assisted conception services and keeper of the post 1991 register.

The Donor Conception Network

The Donor Conception Network provides support and resources to anyone who is thinking about using or who has used egg, sperm or embryo donation to have children. We work directly with families and donor conceived people but also advocate on their behalf, advising clinics, policy makers and other professional bodies.

We are primarily a membership organisation offering contact, community, support and information to donor conception families around the world. Our members range from people at the very early stages of thinking about donor conception to those with adult children now having families of their own.

Our website also provides a wealth of information and guidance. We have an online shop selling books and films for donor conception families including books for young children – the *Our Story* range – and our new book for 8–12yr olds *"Archie Nolan: Family Detective"*.

We publish our Journal twice a year, have a monthly newsletter, run two family conferences in the UK for members each year as well as organising a range of local groups all around the UK. We also offer online contact to members who don't live in the UK or near a local group. We run workshops for those considering donor conception as well as Telling and Talking Workshops for those who have children. Our range of books will continue to expand as our resources allow.

Most importantly we work hard to ensure that donor conception families are represented, their voices are heard, and that donor conception is openly understood by the wider community as one of many ways a family can be created or expanded.

Donor Conception Network

**Join us to be part of an organisation
proudly supporting and championing you
and families like yours.**

**For information about membership or to
make a donation towards our work
please visit our website.**